BIRDS in your BACKYARD

Written and Illustrated by Barbara Herkert

Dawn Publications

Do you know that we share the Earth with about 10,000 different kinds of birds? About 800 different kinds live here in North America. Some of these birds live right outside your backdoor.

Come on, let's take a look and see what's out there!

Do you know the names of the birds in this picture? You can find them in the back of this book.

3

4

Watching birds can be easy and lots of fun.

You can do a few simple things to make your backyard more fun and attractive to birds. Be patient and you may soon see them eating, singing, bathing, nesting, preening and playing.

If you look through binoculars, you can see them as if you are up close—like this **Northern Flicker** that has made a home by digging into a dead tree with its sharp beak. What are the names of the other birds in this picture?

5

Birds need to feel comfortable and safe.
Some kinds of birds need shrubs or trees
where they can escape from danger, or tall grass
where they can hide. These places are where they
build their nests and raise their young. In a city or
suburb, even a single tree or bush can be the perfect
hiding place for birds like this **European Starling**.

Birds need water for drinking and bathing. A birdbath will invite lots of birds to your backyard. You can make your own birdbath with a pie pan or shallow dish. Dig a hole for your pie pan, or put it on a flat surface. Put small rocks or sand at the bottom of the pan to hold it in place and to provide firm footing for the birds. Fill your tiny pond with water. They may come soon after you leave.

Make sure to clean and refill your birdbath often with fresh water, rocks and sand. Birds take baths in other places, too, like garden sprinklers, ponds, puddles, and even leaves covered with rain or dew.

9

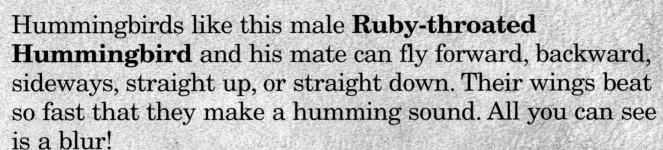

Hummingbirds like this male **Ruby-throated Hummingbird** and his mate can fly forward, backward, sideways, straight up, or straight down. Their wings beat so fast that they make a humming sound. All you can see is a blur!

Birds may eat as much as half their weight in food every day. If you weigh 50 pounds, that would be like eating 25 boxes of cereal every day! Almost all birds eat insects. Many birds eat berries, nuts and seeds. Some drink the nectar from flowers. Others eat earthworms or snails. And some birds hunt for fish, mice or even other birds.

The best way to feed them is to plant trees, bushes and wildflowers that supply food. In the border on page 35 are pictures of some plants that birds especially like.

In the winter, when food is harder to find, it's fun to give them seeds, suet, peanuts, raisins or orange halves. Ask a grown-up to help you fill the bird feeder. Soon birds like these **House Sparrows** and **Black-capped Chickadees** will be flocking outside your door.

12

13

Let's make "cake" for your hungry backyard friends!
Here's what you will need:

1 cup of bird food
   (seeds, nuts, raisins, oats or cornmeal)
½ cup of fat
   (melted lard, suet or vegetable shortening)
½ cup of chunky peanut butter

Ask a grown-up to warm the fat until it melts. Pour the
melted fat into a mixing bowl and add the bird food and
peanut butter. Mix thoroughly. Wait for the mixture to cool.
Then you can smear it into the cracks of trees or pack it into
holes in tree trunks. Another fun way to share this treat is
to spoon it onto a pinecone and hang the pinecone from
a string, or fill hollowed-out orange halves and set
them outside. The birds will gobble their dessert!

Now that birds are flocking to your backyard, how should you go about watching them?

Find a quiet, hidden place where you can see them. Keep a pair of binoculars in your watching spot, and practice focusing them. In cold weather this might be by a window in your house. Remember to keep your voice low and move slowly, even if you're indoors.

You can start a bird journal with a small notebook and some colored pencils. Make a list of every kind you see. It's fun to learn their names—most of the common kinds of birds are shown in the back of this book. Notice each bird's shape, color, and the way it flies. Then draw it or write about it. Listen carefully to their calls—do they sound like words? Write down what you hear. It's also good to write down the date and time you saw them. This is what naturalists do.

A naturalist is an explorer of nature—and that's you! Remember, naturalists are always respectful of nature—we share this backyard home together. Try not to disturb what you watch. Never touch eggs that you find in a nest. Leave baby birds and nesting parents alone. Learn about nature and how to live in harmony with it. Naturalists like you are always seeing or hearing something new, like this **Pine Siskin**.

What kinds of birds will you see in your backyard? If you have a grassy lawn or garden, you are likely to see **American Robins** looking for worms. The female on the ground tilts her head to the side to see better with one eye.

A hungry young robin on top of the post is begging for food from his father. The father is trying to teach the youngster to find food on his own. In addition to worms, robins eat insects and berries. In places where it gets cold in the winter, robins travel south to warmer weather.

"Cheer up, cheerily," they sing.

A mother robin lays three or four bright blue eggs in the spring.

Northern Cardinals often visit bird feeders. Their favorite food is sunflower seeds, but they feed insects to their young. Cardinals build their nests in shrubs or bushes, and the female lays three or four pale green eggs at a time. The males are bright red.

"Cheer, cheer, cheer!" they call.

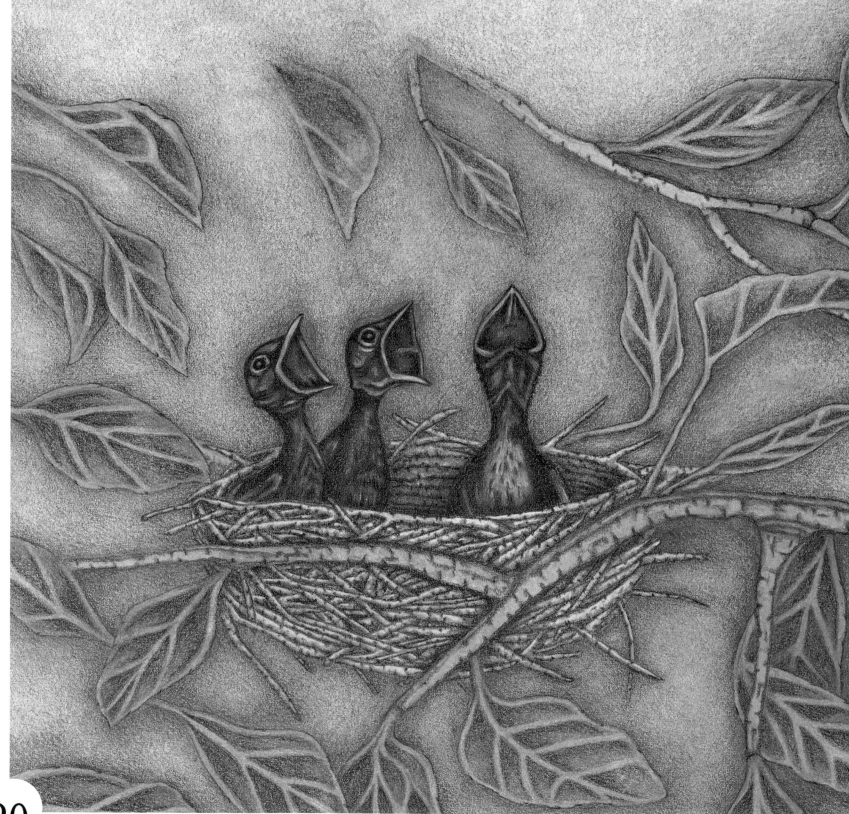

The Northern Cardinal is the official bird of more states than any other bird—Illinois, Indiana, Kentucky, North Carolina, Ohio, Virginia and West Virginia. What is the official bird where you live? Find the answer on pages 32 and 33.

Not long ago, **Eastern Bluebirds** were in trouble! Other birds, such as European Starlings and House Sparrows, would take over their nesting holes and damage their eggs. People started building nest boxes just the right size and shape for bluebirds, and now you may see bluebirds once again, like this female at the entrance, and the male on top.

"Chirrup, chirrup," they sing.

Bluebirds, like many other birds, make seasonal trips called migrations. In late autumn, migrating birds travel thousands of miles south in search of warmer climates and abundant food, and return to more northern climates in the spring.

The Eastern Bluebird has cousins in the West—the **Western Bluebird** (left) and the **Mountain Bluebird** (right).

American Goldfinches like to travel in large flocks, flying together in a wavelike swirl of yellow. In the winter, males and females look pretty much the same, but in the summer the males dress up— they replace their dull coats with a bright yellow coat of feathers and a snappy black cap!

They call, "po-ta-to-chips!" as they fly.

You may see **Downy Woodpeckers** at your birdfeeder, or munching down the bird cake you made. But mostly they eat insects they find on trees. Here, the male is pecking holes in a tree to find bugs inside. They also hollow out big holes in rotting trees to make a nest. Listen for the quick drumming sound they make.

Many other kinds of birds may visit your backyard. In the next few pages are ones you are most likely to find. Which ones do you see outside your backdoor?

American
Crow

American Goldfinch

American
Robin

American Tree Sparrow

Black-capped
Chickadee

White-throated
Sparrow

White-breasted
Nuthatch

Tufted Titmouse

Song Sparrow

Ruby-throated
Hummingbird

Common Backyard Birds

Every bird is an individual, so don't expect the birds in your yard to look exactly like the pictures in this book. The way birds appear also changes with the seasons, with age, with location, and whether the bird is male or female.

Grown youngsters of **American Crows** may help with making the nest and raising the new nestlings.

The male **American Goldfinch** will feed the female as she sits on her eggs.

American Robins may run at each other with their heads lowered, as if to say, "Back off! This is my territory!"

American Tree Sparrows say "Whee-hee-ho-hee" and "Tseet!" They line the inside of their nests with animal fur.

A **Black-capped Chickadee** opens a sunflower seed by holding it in his feet and cracking it with his bill.

Blue Jays can get rowdy at bird feeders, chasing other birds away. They may fill their throat pouches with seeds and fly off to hide them under the bark of trees.

Brown-headed Cowbirds lay their eggs in the nests of other birds. The other birds sit on the eggs and raise the young cowbirds as their own!

The **Carolina Chickadee** eats the berries of poison ivy.

Carolina Wrens build their nests in funny places—like mailboxes or the pocket of a pair of pants hanging from a clothesline!

The **Common Grackle** may dunk his food in a birdbath before eating it.

Dark-eyed Juncos are also known as snowbirds, because they visit bird feeders in the winter. "Kew-kew-kew-kew!" they call.

When you hear a **Downy Woodpecker** drumming against a tree, it's a good sign that winter will soon end. "Peek!" they call.

The **Eastern Towhee** is also known as a swamp robin, ground robin, marsh robin, bullfinch, bushbird, and turkey sparrow. Its call sounds like "Sip your tea!"

European Starlings can fly up to 55 miles an hour—that's twice as fast as most of the birds in your backyard.

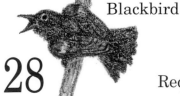

Red-winged
Blackbird

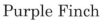

Red-breasted Nuthatch

Purple Finch

Pine Siskin

Northern Flicker
(Yellow-
shafted)

Blue Jay

Brown-headed Cowbird

Carolina Chickadee

Carolina Wren

Common Grackle

Dark-eyed (Slate-colored) Junco

Downy Woodpecker

# of Eastern North America

Evening Grosbeaks use their large, heavy bill to open seeds.

Sometimes **Hairy Woodpeckers**, like all kinds of woodpeckers, drum on tree limbs to say, "This is my territory!"

In the eastern U.S., **House Finches** got their start as pet birds, until some pet shop owners set them free.

House Sparrows build their nests with grass, weeds, leaves, even trash!

The **Mourning Dove's** call is a soft, cooing sound.

A **Northern Cardinal** father watches over the baby birds while the mother bird makes a new nest.

Northern Flicker nestlings make a humming noise if disturbed, which sometimes sounds like a swarm of bees.

Pine Siskins are acrobats, often hanging upside down to pluck seeds from plants and bird feeders.

Purple Finches are not really purple. Males are a rosy red color; females and young birds are a duller brown and white striped.

The **Red-breasted Nuthatch** makes a sound like "Nyank, nyank!"

Red-winged Blackbirds sound like they are saying "Conk-a-ree!"

The eggs of the **Ruby-throated Hummingbird** are about the size of a pea.

In the spring, male **Song Sparrows** spend much of their day singing while fluffing their feathers and waving one or both wings.

The call of the **Tufted Titmouse** sounds like "Pe-ter, Pe-ter!"

White-breasted Nuthatches have strong toes and claws that grip the bark as they walk head-first down trees. They rarely come to the ground.

White-throated Sparrows sound like they are saying "Old Sam Peabody, Peabody, Peabody."

Eastern (Rufous-sided) Towhee

European Starling

Evening Grosbeak

Hairy Woodpecker

Northern Cardinal

Mourning Dove

House Sparrow

House Finch

American
Crow

American Goldfinch

American
Robin

Anna's Hummingbird

Black-capped
Chickadee

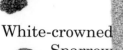
White-crowned
Sparrow

White-breasted
Nuthatch

Varied
Thrush

Steller's
Jay

Spotted (Rufous-sided) Towhee

Song Sparrow

Common Backyard Birds

Every bird is an individual, so don't expect the birds in your yard to look exactly like the pictures in this book. The way birds appear also changes with the seasons, with age, with location, and whether the bird is male or female.

Listen to the familiar "Caw, caw" of the **American Crow**—his call may mean different things, such as "Danger is near" or "I found food!"

American Goldfinches strengthen their nests with spider or caterpillar webs and line them with thistledown. The nests are so tightly woven, they can even hold water.

Young **American Robins** grow up fast. Just 14 days after hatching, they are almost as big as their parents!

Anna's Hummingbird likes to build its nest above water. Parents feed their baby birds insects that hover over the stream or pond.

Black-capped Chickadees are so curious that they will sometimes eat right out of your hand!

You may see **Brewer's Blackbirds** in suburban parks, freeway plantings or parking lots. It sounds like they are saying "Check!"

A **Cassin's Finch** sounds like "Pwee-de-lip!" These rose and brown-streaked birds make their homes in tall firs and pines.

The **Chestnut-backed Chickadee** makes holes in rotten stumps and then builds a nest of moss and hair inside.

Dark-eyed Juncos like to feed and make their nests on the ground.

A **Downy Woodpecker's** long tongue has tiny hooks on the end for spearing insects.

The **European Starling's** bill is bright yellow in the spring and summer, but in the winter it turns dark.

Evening Grosbeaks may come to your bird feeder in large, noisy flocks.

Golden-crowned Sparrows make their nests on or near the ground. Parent birds must be on the lookout for many dangers, including bullfrogs!

A father **Hairy Woodpecker** will often make himself a "bedroom" in a tree next door to the nest.

Red-breasted Nuthatch

Scrub
Jay

Red-winged
Blackbird

Purple Finch

Pine Siskin

Brewer's Blackbird

Cassin's Finch

Chestnut-backed Chickadee

Dark-eyed (Oregon) Junco

Dark-eyed (Pink-sided) Junco

Downy Woodpecker

# of Western North America

House Finches will nest almost anywhere—in flowerpots, on building ledges or in other birds' nests. Their call sounds like "Wheet!"

Like many other birds, **House Sparrows** take baths often, sometimes even in the dirt!

Mountain Chickadees, like Black-capped Chickadees, will often eat right from your hand.

If you listen carefully when a **Mourning Dove** flies, you can hear the whistling noise of their wings.

Northern Flickers sound like they are calling their own name—"Flicka-flicka-flicka!"

Pine Siskins are tiny but feisty! They are not above stealing seeds from other birds at bird feeders.

If you are tardy about refilling your bird feeder, **Purple Finches** will complain to you about it. Their call sounds like "Cheer-lee!"

The **Red-breasted Nuthatch** climbs down trees head first!

When they migrate, **Red-winged Blackbirds** group together in large flocks. They sound like they are saying "Conk-a-ree!"

Scrub Jays bury many more acorns than they can eat. They help plant new oak trees, especially in areas where forests have been destroyed by fire or drought.

Song Sparrows are well known for their beautiful songs. Male birds may sing up to ten different songs.

Spotted Towhees search for food by hopping backwards and forwards, scratching the ground with their feet.

The **Steller's Jay** wears a large black crested hat of feathers. Listen to him shriek "Shack-shack-shack-shack!"

You may hear the **Varied Thrush's** buzzing song before you see him—he's likely to be hiding high in a tree.

The **White-breasted Nuthatch** will wedge seeds in the cracks of trees and then peck to open them. He has just the right bill for the job—it's long and sharp.

When **White-crowned Sparrows** gather together before migrating to warmer weather, they seem to whisper to each other in a wheezy whistle.

European Starling

Evening Grosbeak

Fox Sparrow

Golden-crowned Sparrow

Hairy Woodpecker

Northern Flicker (Red-shafted)

Mourning Dove

House Sparrow

House Finch

Mountain Chickadee

Northern Flicker (Yellowhammer)

Willow Ptarmigan

Cactus Wren

Northern Mockingbird

California Quail

Lark Bunting

Sharp-tailed Grouse

Snowy Owl

Gyrfalcon

Great Grey Owl

Stellar's Jay

Great Horned Owl

Osprey

Raven

State Birds of the United States

Alabama—Northern Flicker (Yellowhammer)
Alaska—Willow Ptarmigan
Arizona—Cactus Wren
Arkansas—Northern Mockingbird
California—California Quail
Colorado—Lark Bunting
Connecticut—American Robin
Delaware—Blue Hen Chicken
Florida—Northern Mockingbird
Georgia—Brown Thrasher
Hawaii—Hawaiian Goose
Idaho—Mountain Bluebird
Illinois—Northern Cardinal
Indiana—Northern Cardinal
Iowa—American Goldfinch
Kansas—Western Meadowlark
Kentucky—Northern Cardinal
Louisiana—Brown Pelican
Maine—Black-capped Chickadee
Maryland—Baltimore Oriole
Massachusetts—Black-capped Chickadee
Michigan—American Robin
Minnesota—Common Loon
Mississippi—Northern Mockingbird
Missouri—Eastern Bluebird
Montana—Western Meadowlark
Nebraska—Western Meadowlark
Nevada—Mountain Bluebird
New Hampshire—Purple Finch
New Jersey—American Goldfinch
New Mexico—Greater Roadrunner
New York—Eastern Bluebird
North Carolina—Northern Cardinal
North Dakota—Western Meadowlark
Ohio—Northern Cardinal
Oklahoma—Scissor-tailed Flycatcher
Oregon—Western Meadowlark
Pennsylvania—Ruffed Grouse
Rhode Island—Rhode Island Red Chicken
South Carolina—Carolina Wren
South Dakota—Ring-necked Pheasant
Tennessee—Northern Mockingbird
Texas—Northern Mockingbird
Utah—California Gull
Vermont—Hermit Thrush
Virginia—Northern Cardinal
Washington—American Goldfinch
West Virginia—Northern Cardinal
Wisconsin—American Robin
Wyoming—Western Meadowlark

Alaska

Yukon Territory

North Territory

Nunavu

British Columbia

Alberta

Saskatchewan

Washington

Oregon

California

Nevada

Idaho

Utah

Arizona

Montana

Wyoming

Colorado

New Mexico

Nort Dako

South Dako

Nebras

Kan

Oklaho

Texa

Mexico

Great Horned Owl

Hermit Thrush

California Gull

Ring-necked Pheasant

Carolina Wren

Rhode Island Red Chicken

32

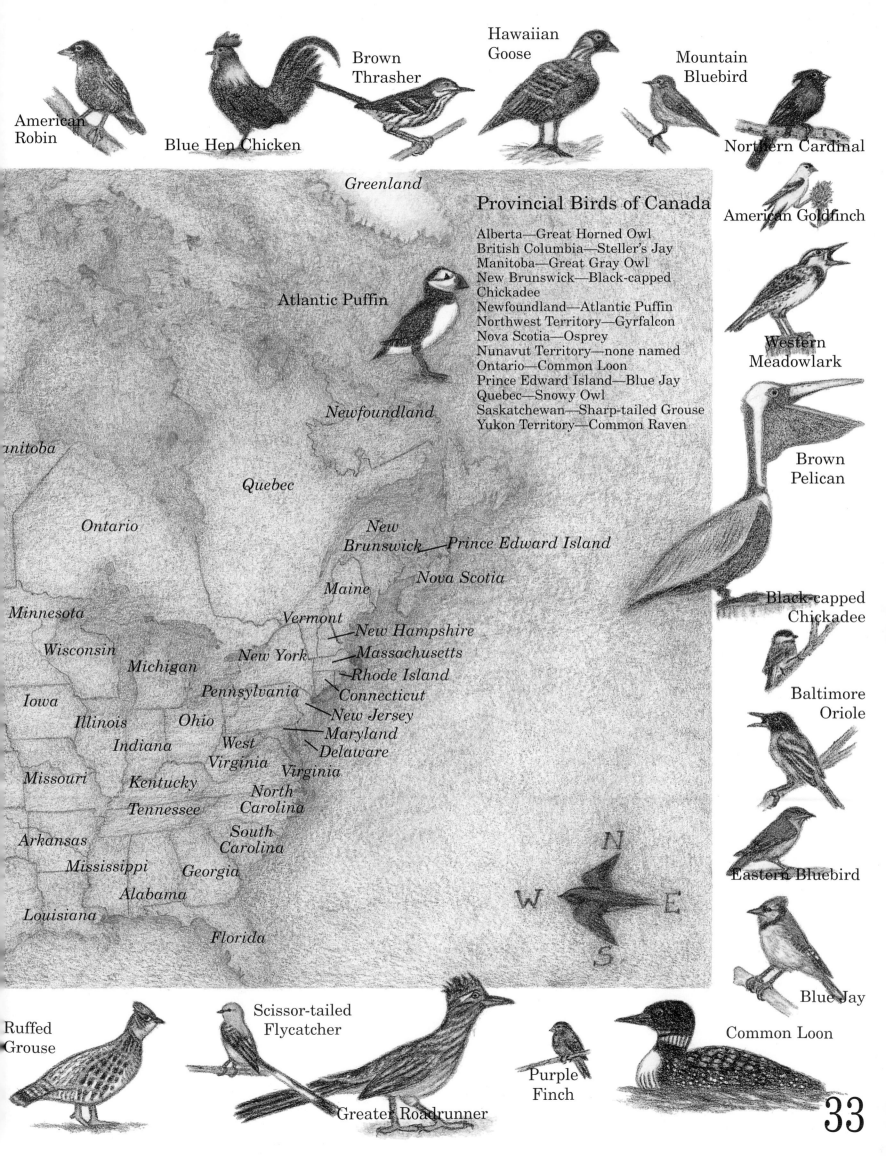

American Robin

Blue Hen Chicken

Brown Thrasher

Hawaiian Goose

Mountain Bluebird

Northern Cardinal

American Goldfinch

Western Meadowlark

Brown Pelican

Black-capped Chickadee

Baltimore Oriole

Eastern Bluebird

Blue Jay

Greenland

Atlantic Puffin

Newfoundland

Provincial Birds of Canada

Alberta—Great Horned Owl
British Columbia—Steller's Jay
Manitoba—Great Gray Owl
New Brunswick—Black-capped Chickadee
Newfoundland—Atlantic Puffin
Northwest Territory—Gyrfalcon
Nova Scotia—Osprey
Nunavut Territory—none named
Ontario—Common Loon
Prince Edward Island—Blue Jay
Quebec—Snowy Owl
Saskatchewan—Sharp-tailed Grouse
Yukon Territory—Common Raven

Manitoba

Quebec

Ontario

New Brunswick — Prince Edward Island

Nova Scotia

Maine

Minnesota

Wisconsin

Vermont

New Hampshire

New York

Massachusetts

Rhode Island

Michigan

Connecticut

Pennsylvania

New Jersey

Iowa

Maryland

Illinois

Ohio

Delaware

Indiana

West Virginia

Virginia

Missouri

Kentucky

Tennessee

North Carolina

Arkansas

South Carolina

Mississippi

Georgia

Alabama

Louisiana

Florida

N
W E
S

Ruffed Grouse

Scissor-tailed Flycatcher

Greater Roadrunner

Purple Finch

Common Loon

House Wren
Entrance size: 1" to 1¼"
Height: 4' to 10'

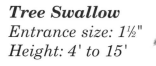

Tree Swallow
Entrance size: 1½"
Height: 4' to 15'

Mountain Bluebird
Entrance size: 1⁹⁄₁₆"
Height: 3'-6'

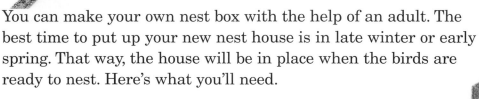

Black-capped Chickadee
Entrance size: 1⅛"
Height: 4' to 15'

Red-breasted Nuthatch
Entrance size: 1¼"
Height: 12'-20'

You can make your own nest box with the help of an adult. The best time to put up your new nest house is in late winter or early spring. That way, the house will be in place when the birds are ready to nest. Here's what you'll need.

- 1" x 5" pine board, 2 feet long
- 1" x 6" pine board, 3 feet long
- ruler
- saw
- drill with a 1½" and a ¼" bit
- galvanized nails
- hammer
- square bend hook

1. Measure and mark the cutting lines on the two boards as shown. Mark the locations of the entrance hole, ventilation holes and the hole by which you will hang your nesting box as shown in the diagram.

2. Have an adult cut the board with a saw and drill the entrance hole using the 1½" bit. Drill the hanging hole and ventilation holes with the ¼" bit.

3. On the back of the front piece, scratch some deep horizontal lines under the entrance hole with one of the nails. These grooves will make it easier for young birds to climb out of the box when they are ready to leave the nest.

4. Nail the pieces together with the help of an adult, leaving one side not nailed at the bottom. Screw the square bend hook into the bottom of this side. This will allow it to swing open so that you can clean out the nesting box when the birds have left the nest.

Eastern Bluebird
Entrance size: 1½"
Height: 3' to 6'

Downy Woodpecker
Entrance size: 1¼"
Height: 5' to 15'

Mountain Chickadee
Entrance size 1⅛"
Height: 4'-15'

Western Bluebird
Entrance size: 1½"
Height: 3'-6'

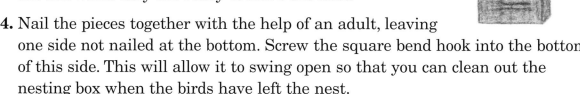

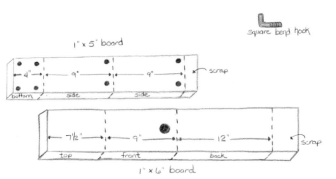

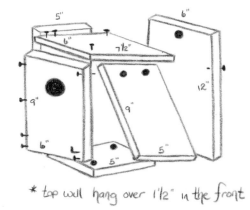

----- = cutting lines

• = ventilation holes (¼")

● = entrance hole (1½")

* top will hang over 1½" in the front

Used with permission from Bird Tales from Near & Far by Susan Milord ©1998, Williamson Publishing, Charlotte, VT

Tufted Titmouse
Entrance size: 1¼"
Height: 5' to 15'

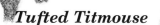

White-breasted Nuthatch
Entrance size: 1¼"
Height: 12' to 20'

Carolina Wren
Entrance size: 1½"
Height: 5' to 10'

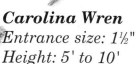

American Elm

Columbine

Staghorn Sumac

Mountain Ash

Azalea

Beech

White Oak

Juniper

Columbia
Hawthorne

Strawberry

Fuchsia

Serviceberry

In the border are illustrations of plants that birds particularly like.

Resources

Books

The Audubon Society First Field Guide is published especially for children. The Society's *Field Guides to North American Birds* are for adults, but the photographs provide easy identification for children.

Backyard Birds (Peterson Field Guides for Young Naturalists), written for children ages 9 to 12, introduces the Roger Tory Peterson method of bird identification.

Bird Tales from Near & Far by Susan Milord and *Birdhouses & Feeders* by Robyn Haus have both stories and hands-on projects. Williamson Publishing Co., 800-234-8791

Organizations

The American Birding Association offers several programs for young birders, including A Bird's-Eye View, a bimonthly newsletter, and distributes information on many birding events suitable for families. Call (800) 850-2473 or (719) 578-9703, or visit www.americanbirding.org

The Audubon Society offers many educational materials for classroom or home use, including Audubon Adventures (www.audubon.org/educate), an environmental education program for grades 4-6, and WatchList 4 Kids (www.audubon.org/bird/watch/kids), which enables children to help scientists by studying bird population trends.

The Cornell Lab of Ornithology has several science projects, including the Birdhouse Network, and Project FeederWatch. Educators may be interested in Classroom FeederWatch, a research and interdisciplinary education curriculum designed for grades 5-8. Go to www.birds.cornell.edu or call 800-843-2473 (607-254-2473 from outside the U.S.)

The National Wildlife Federation provides materials and training for parents, teachers and communities interested in creating and restoring wildlife habitat in their backyards and on their school grounds (in the case of schools, incorporating the habitat into their curriculum). Backyards or schools may apply for certification as an official Backyard or Schoolyard Habitat site. Call 703-438-6000, visit www.nwf.org or write:

National Wildlife Federation
11100 Wildlife Center Drive
Reston, VA 20190

A Note On Binoculars:

When buying a pair of binoculars for young children, look for a pair that is small, light weight, rugged, and easy to focus. They should have a low magnification power of about four (the first number in, say, a 4 X 30 pair) to make it easy to hold steady, and a wide field of vision (the second number) to make it easy to find things. For an older child with an interest in birdwatching, you may wish to invest more for better optical quality.

American Holly

Eastern Red Cedar

White Mulberry

Flowering Dogwood

Viburnum

White Spruce

Crab Apple

Bayberry

Wild Grape

About the Author/Illustrator

Photo by Donna McCoy

As a young girl accompanied by her dad, Barbara Herkert watched the birds in her backyard. Now with her two children, she daily rediscovers the wonders of nature. Barbara's background is in both biology and fine art. She shares her home in Newport, Oregon, with her husband Greg, and children Keith and Jenna, two dogs, two birds, two tortoises, a variety of fish and a very old hamster. This is her first picture book.

Acknowledgments

Many thanks to Craig Tufts and Dave Mizejewski of the National Wildlife Federation's Backyard Wildlife Habitat program; Matt Pelikan of the American Birding Association; and Allison Childs Wells of the Cornell Lab of Ornithology's Project FeederWatch, all of whom with great courtesy provided valuable information. And thank you to photographer Michael Goss and CLICK magazine for the photo reference from the January 1998 cover.

Dedication

For my family, for their never ending love and support, and for backyard naturalists everywhere.

ABOUT THE SHARING NATURE WITH CHILDREN BOOKS

Each book in the Sharing Nature with Children series from Dawn Publications encourages in children a positive connection with nature. Once that connection is made, nature inspires science, literature, and a lifetime of inspiration. The following are a few titles from this collection. A complete catalog is available upon request.

My Favorite Tree by Diane Iverson. A young person's guide to North American trees shows a child engaged with each major tree family in some way, along with a clear but simple explanation of its major features, history, and wildlife companions.

Under One Rock: Bugs, Slugs and Other Ughs by Anthony Fredericks, visits the community of creatures that all live together under a rock.

This is the Sea that Feeds Us by Robert F. Baldwin. In simple cumulative verse, this book explores the oceans' fabulous food chain that reaches from plankton to whales and humans in an intricate web.

Salmon Stream by Carol Reed-Jones. Against staggering odds, salmon hatch and grow, travel to the ocean, and eventually struggle upstream to their birthplace again. The cumulative verse connects each event.

Earth & You—A Closer View: Nature's Features and **Earth & Us—Continuous: Nature's Past and Future** by J. Patrick Lewis. With lyrical sweep and luxuriously detailed illustrations, these books promote a global awareness of nature.

Stickeen: John Muir and the Brave Little Dog by Donnell Rubay. This is the classic story of John Muir's true adventure with a little dog on an Alaskan glacier that transformed their relationship and gave Muir a "window" through which he could see into the heart of the animal kingdom.

A Swim Through the Sea, A Walk in the Rainforest, and **A Fly in the Sky** comprise the popular trilogy of habitat books written and illustrated by the young author, Kristin Joy Pratt-Serafini. Each book presents its habitat in alphabetical and alliterative format.

A Drop Around the World, by Barbara Shaw McKinney, follows a single drop of water—from snow to steam, from polluted to purified, from stratus cloud to subterranean crack. Drop inspires our respect for water's unique role on Earth.

A Tree in the Ancient Forest, by Carol Reed-Jones, uses repetitive, cumulative verse to show graphically the remarkable web of interdependent plants and animals that all call a big old tree home.

Dawn Publications
P.O. Box 2010
Nevada City, CA 95959
530-478-0111
nature@dawnpub.com

Dawn Publications is dedicated to inspiring in children a deeper understanding and appreciation for all life on Earth. To order, or for a copy of our catalog, please call 800-545-7475. Please also visit our web site at www.dawnpub.com.